COMPOSER SHOWCASE
HAL LEONARD STUDENT PIANO LIBRARY

Sea Diary

NINE ORIGINAL PIANO SOLOS

BY CHRISTOS TSITSAROS

T0071262

To my precious mother, Violetta, whose love and care nourished and gave me limitless encouragement, support, and artistic inspiration. This *Sea Diary* brings me back to my childhood years, when seated around the dinner table, my mother would suggest wonderful descriptive ideas and poetic images that I included in my school essays. She would open the large curtain of the world for me and I was delighted in getting to know this world through her guidance.

I carry in my heart her grace, kindness, and beauty, in thankful recognition of all she did for me and the rest of my family.

ISBN 978-1-5400-1335-4

7777 W. BLUEMOUND RD. P.O. BOX 13819 MILWAUKEE, WI 53213

In Australia Contact:
Hal Leonard Australia Pty. Ltd.
4 Lentara Court
Cheltenham, Victoria, 3192 Australia
Email: ausadmin@halleonard.com.au

Visit Hal Leonard Online at
www.halleonard.com

CONTENTS

NOTES FROM THE COMPOSER

The pieces of the *Sea Diary* were composed at various intervals during the summer and fall of 2015, while on sabbatical leave in my native country, Cyprus. Their inspiration came from the breathtaking landscape that surrounded me in the port city of Larnaca, where I lived during the entire period.

The strikingly unique and varied seascape absorbed my imagination to the extent that I felt compelled to keep a musical diary of all my vivid impressions. Not confined to words, I could jot down my feelings and thoughts more subtly and accurately in sounds. Over time, this emotional blending with nature deepened: I found a translation of my inner world in the seascape's manifold aspects, such as the morning clamor of the harbor, the bravado of a fisherman who is about to set sail, the sense of urgency at the sight of gathering clouds before a storm, and the quiet contemplation of a lone shell lying in the sand. All these images resonated deeply in me. The entire experience was heightened by the magnificent display of colors in the sky, the bright morning blue progressively giving way to the blazing sunset gold, followed by the impalpable lavender and pink hues of the late afternoon. The plaintive sounds of seagulls leaving for their faraway journey in the early autumn completed the perfection of this evocative canvas.

I had discovered an indescribable, blessed internal quiet that allowed a total connection within myself and with nature. I hope that by letting the musical thread transport them to the lively scenes of this diary, young students will be able to relate to my spiritual experiences through their own imagination.

–Christos Tsitsaros

A Lonely, Empty Shell

By Christos Tsitsaros

An Approaching Storm

By Christos Tsitsaros

Rather fast, with a sense of unrest

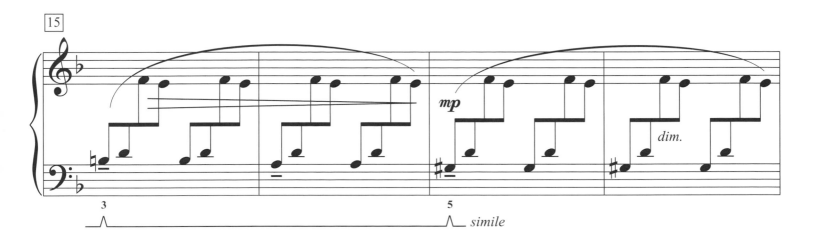

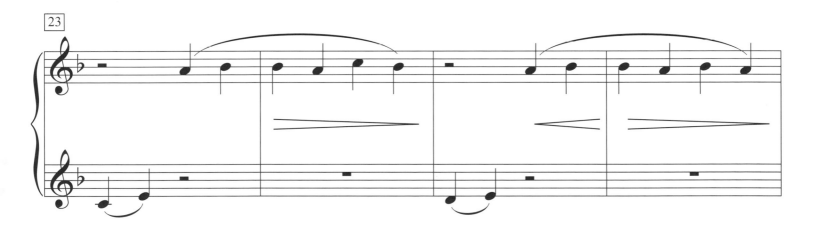

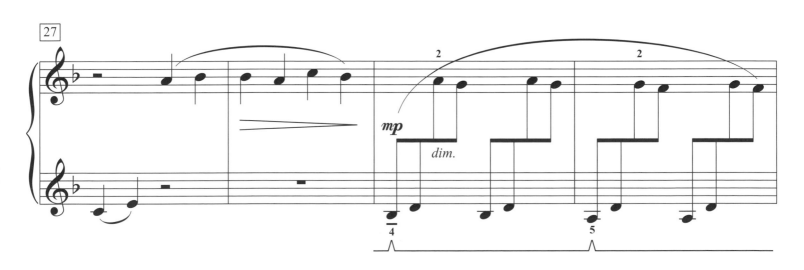

The Bustling Harbor

By Christos Tsitsaros

Rather fast, with boldnesss

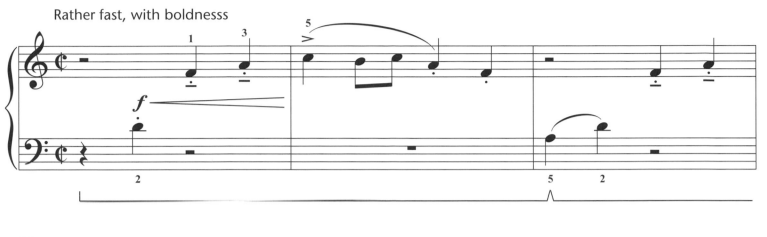

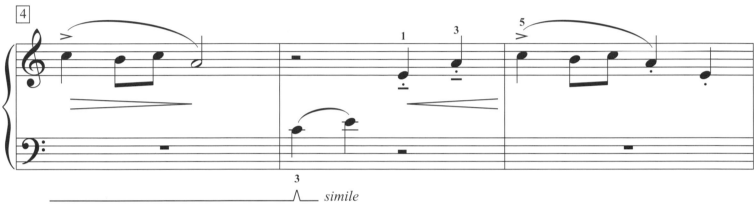

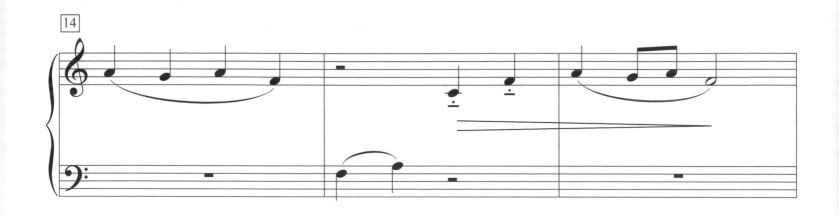

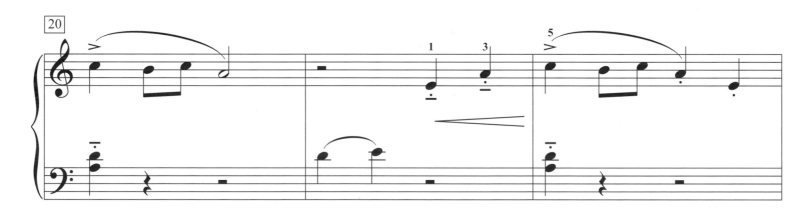

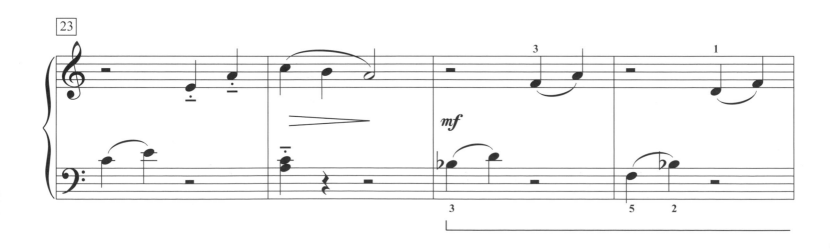

poco dim.

mp

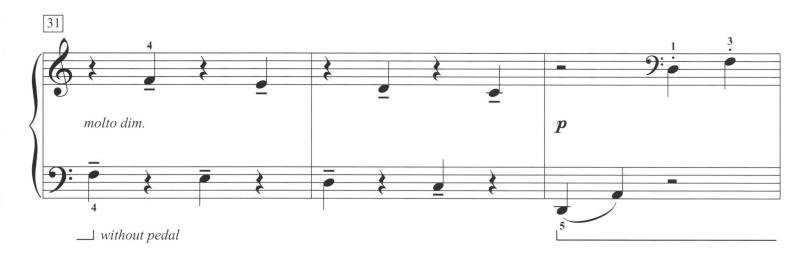

molto dim.

p

⌐⌐ without pedal

simile

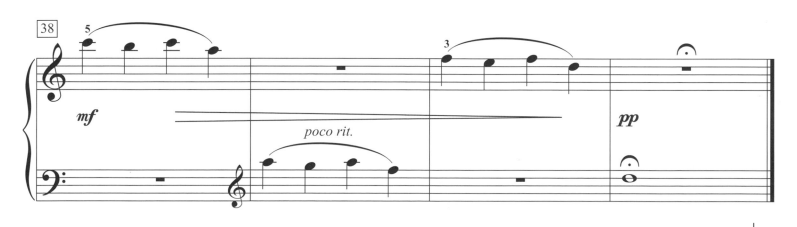

mf

poco rit.

pp

Late Afternoon on the Shore

By Christos Tsitsaros

Moderately slow, with motion

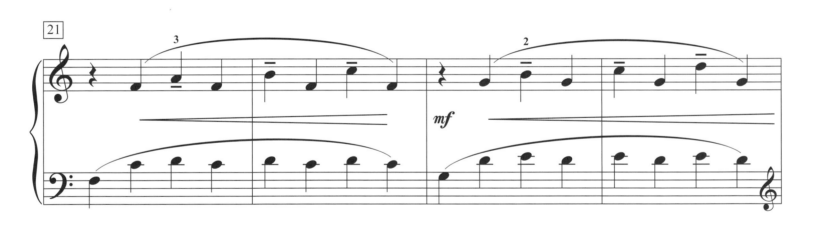

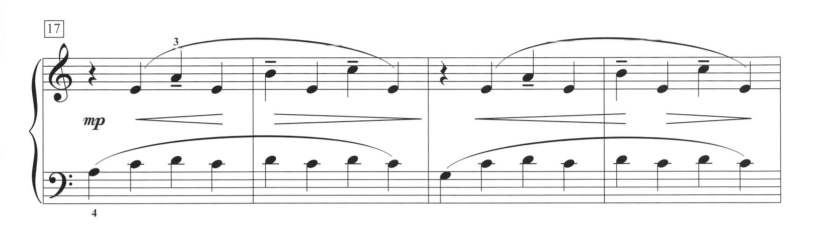

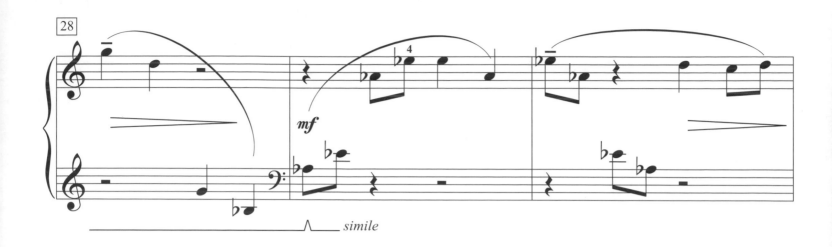

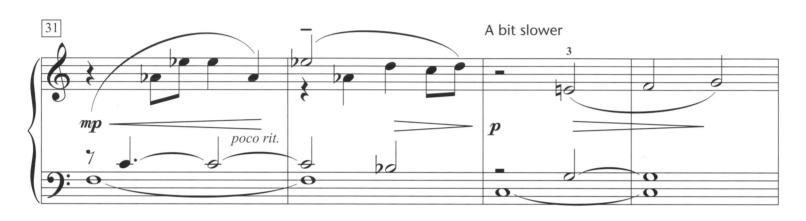

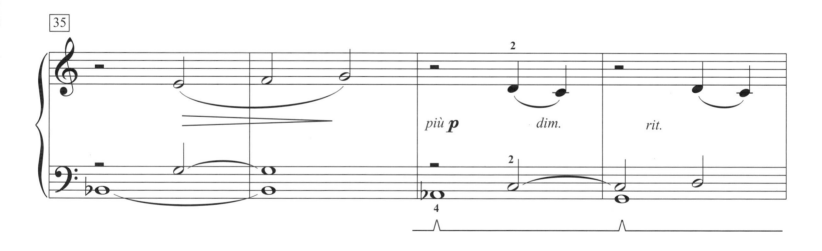

Song of the Brave Fisherman

By Christos Tsitsaros

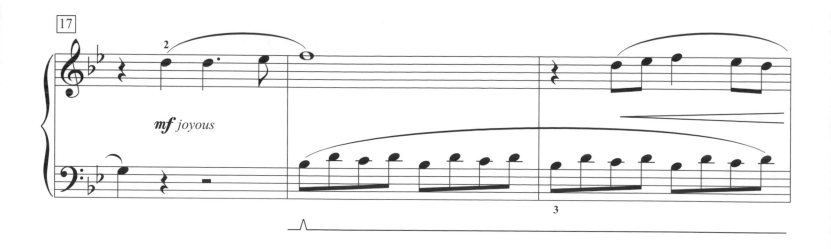

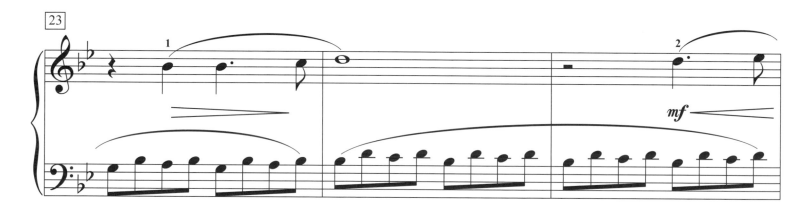

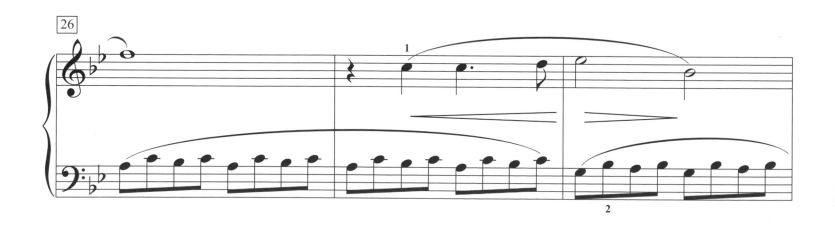

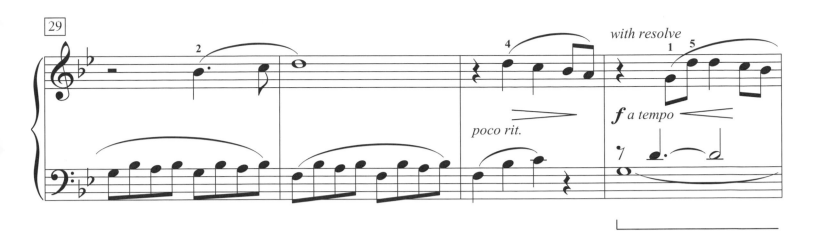

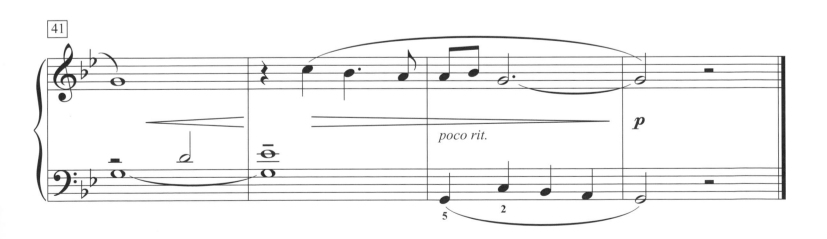

Red Kites in the Blue Sky

By Christos Tsitsaros

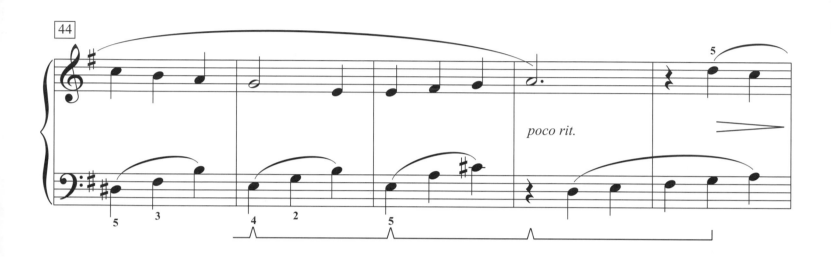

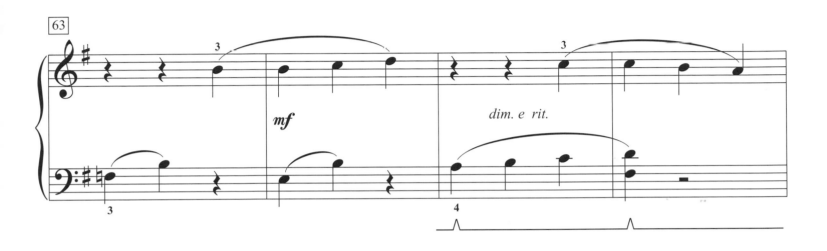

Seascape with Falling Sun

By Christos Tsitsaros

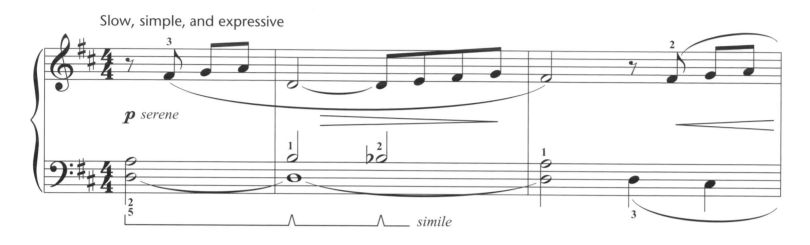

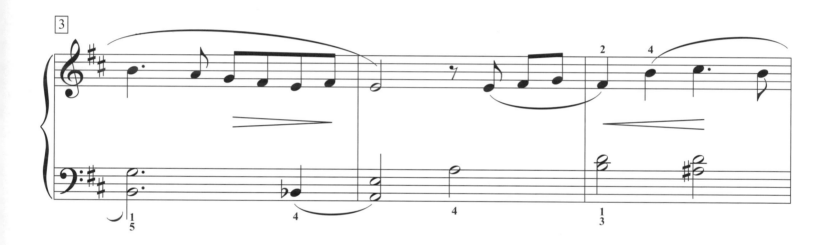

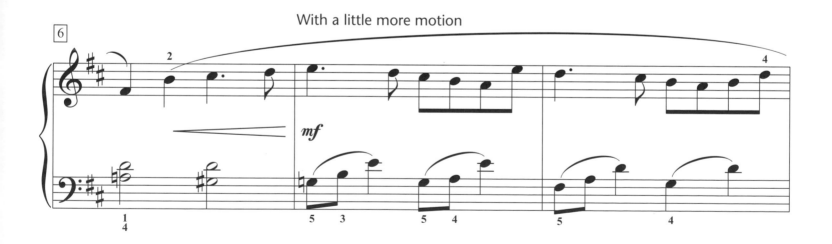

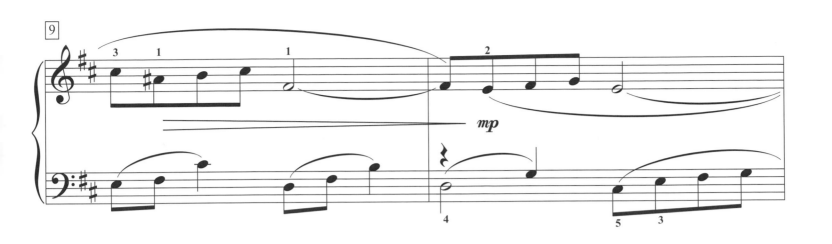

Slower and majestic

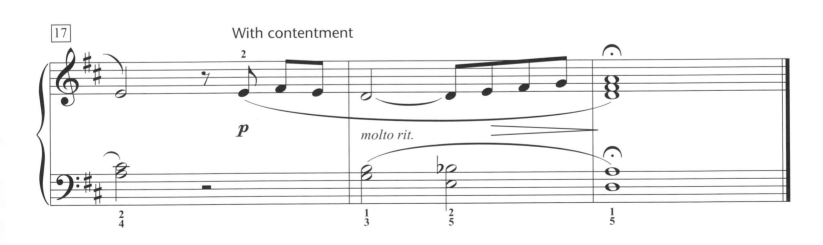

With contentment

23

The Wondering Whale
(Toccata)

By Christos Tsitsaros

Allegro con spirito

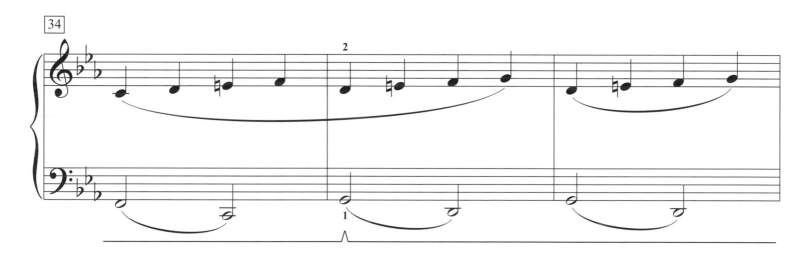

The Seagulls' Farewell

By Christos Tsitsaros

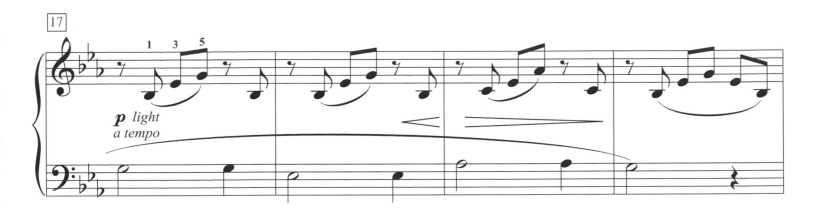

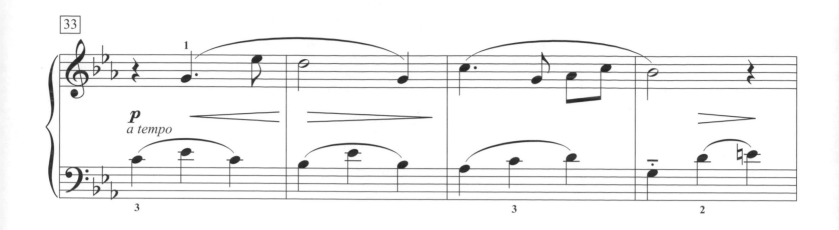

CHRISTOS TSITSAROS

Christos Tsitsaros, contributing composer and arranger for the *Hal Leonard Student Piano Library*, is Professor and Chairman of the Piano Pedagogy division of the University of Illinois at Urbana-Champaign. A native of Cyprus, he won first prize at the *Keti Papaioannou National Piano Competition* of the Conservatory of Athens at age 13. He continued his musical studies at the Frédéric Chopin Academy of Warsaw and later in Paris, at the École Normale (Diplôme Supérieur d Exécution), the Jacobs School of Music of Indiana University (Artist Diploma, Master's), and the University of Illinois (Doctor of Musical Arts in Piano Performance, 1993).

A winner of the 1992 composition competition of the *National Conference on Piano Pedagogy*, he served as clinician and lecturer for NCKP, the *Music Teachers National Association Conference*, the *International Conference on European Music Education* (St. Petersburg, Russia), and was featured artist for the 2013 *Symposium on Piano Pedagogy* in Seoul, South Korea. He was also artist-in-residence at the *Helene Wurlitzer Foundation* (2001) and the 2014 Piano Competition of the University of Texas in El Paso. He has appeared as recitalist and chamber musician in Europe and the United States. In 2014, Dr. Tsitsaros was honored as the "Distinguished Composer of the Year" by the Music Teachers National Association for his *Three Preludes for Solo Piano: a Mythical Triptych*. More recently, he was commissioned composer for the 2017 MTNA National Conference in Baltimore, Maryland, where his *Fantasy* trio for oboe, B-flat clarinet, and piano was performed (*From the Pen to the Premiere*). Four individual albums of his piano works appear under the *Centaur Records* label (1998, 2007, 2011).

Piano Recital Showcase

"What should my students play for the recital?" This series provides easy answers to this common question. For these winning collections, we've carefully selected some of the most popular and effective pieces from the **Hal Leonard Student Library** – from early-elementary to late-intermediate levels. You'll love the variety of musical styles found in each book.

PIANO RECITAL SHOWCASE PRE-STAFF

Pre-Staff Early Elementary Level
8 solos: Bumper Cars • Cherokee Lullaby • Fire Dance • The Hungry Spider • On a Magic Carpet • One, Two, Three • Pickled Pepper Polka • Pumpkin Song.
00296784 ....$7.99

BOOK 1

Elementary Level
12 solos: B.B.'s Boogie • In My Dreams • Japanese Garden • Jazz Jig • Joyful Bells • Lost Treasure • Monster March • Ocean Breezes • Party Cat Parade • Rainy Day Play • Sledding Fun • Veggie Song.
00296749 ....$8.99

BOOK 2

Late-Elementary Level
12 solos: Angelfish Arabesque • The Brontosaurus Bop • From the Land of Make-Believe • Ghosts of a Sunken Pirate Ship • The Happy Walrus • Harvest Dance • Hummingbird (L'oiseau-mouche) • Little Bird • Quick Spin in a Fast Car • Shifty-Eyed Blues • The Snake Charmer • Soft Shoe Shuffle.
00296748 ....$7.99

BOOK 3

Intermediate Level
10 solos: Castilian Dreamer • Dreaming Song • Jump Around Rag • Little Mazurka • Meaghan's Melody • Mountain Splendor • Seaside Stride • Snap to It! • Too Cool to Fool • Wizard's Wish.
00296747 ....$8.99

BOOK 4

Late-Intermediate Level
8 solos: Berceuse for Janey • Cafe Waltz • Forever in My Heart • Indigo Bay • Salsa Picante • Sassy Samba • Skater's Dream • Twilight on the Lake.
00296746 ....$8.99

CHRISTMAS EVE SOLOS

Intermediate Level
Composed for the intermediate level student, these pieces provide fresh and substantial repertoire for students not quite ready for advanced piano literature. Includes: Auld Lang Syne • Bring a Torch, Jeannette, Isabella • Coventry Carol • O Little Town of Bethlehem • Silent Night • We Wish You a Merry Christmas • and more.
00296877...$8.99

DUET FAVORITES

Intermediate Level
Five original duets for one piano, four hands from top composers Phillip Keveren, Eugénie Rocherolle, Sondra Clark and Wendy Stevens. Includes: Angel Falls • Crescent City Connection • Prime Time • A Wind of Promise • Yearning.
00296898...$9.99

FESTIVAL FAVORITES, BOOK 1
10 OUTSTANDING NFMC SELECTED SOLOS

Late Elementary/Early Intermediate Level
Proven piano solos fill this compilation of selected gems chosen for various National Federation of Music Clubs (NFMC) Junior Festival lists. Titles: Candlelight Prelude • Crazy Man's Blues • I've Gotta Toccata • Pagoda Bells • Tarantella • Toccata Festivo • Tonnerre sur les plaines (Thunder on the Plains) • Twister • Way Cool! • Wild Robot.
00118198...$10.99

FESTIVAL FAVORITES, BOOK 2
10 OUTSTANDING NFMC SELECTED SOLOS

Intermediate/Late Intermediate Level
Book 2 features: Barcarolle Impromptu • Cathedral Echoes (Harp Song) • Dance of the Trolls • Jasmine in the Mist • Jesters • Maestro, There's a Fly in My Waltz • Mother Earth, Sister Moon • Northwoods Toccata • Sounds of the Rain • Un phare dans le brouillard (A Lighthouse in the Fog).
00118202...$10.99

FESTIVAL GEMS – BOOK 1

Elementary/Late Elementary Level
This convenient collection features 10 NFMC-selected piano solos: Brooklyn's Waltz • Chimichanga Cha-Cha • Feelin' Happy • Footprints in the Snow • Lazy Daisy • New Orleans Jamboree • PBJ Blues • Pepperoni Pizza • Sneakin' Cake • Things That Go Bump in the Night. (Note: Solos are from previous NFMC lists.)
00193548 ....$10.99

FESTIVAL GEMS – BOOK 2

Early Intermediate/Intermediate Level
Book 2 includes: Caravan • Chatterbox • In the Groove • Jubilation! • Kokopelli (Invention in Phrygian Mode) • La marée de soir (Evening Tide) • Reverie • Time Travel • Voiliers dans le vent (Sailboats in the Wind) • Williwaw.
00193587 ....$10.99

FESTIVAL GEMS – BOOK 3

Late Intermediate/Early Advanced Level
8 more NFMC-selected piano solos, including: Cuentos Del Matador (Tales of the Matador) • Daffodil Caprice • Love Song in the Rain • Midnight Prayer • Nocturne d'Esprit • Rapsodie • Scherzo • Urban Heartbeat.
00193588 ....$10.99

RAGTIME!

Early Intermediate/Intermediate Level
8 original rags from Bill Boyd, Phillip Keveren, Carol Klose, Jennifer Linn, Mona Rejino, Christos Tsitsaros and Jennifer & Mike Watts are featured in this solo piano collection. Includes: Butterfly Rag • Carnival Rag • Jump Around Rag • Nashville Rag • Ragtime Blue • St. Louis Rag • Swingin' Rag • Techno Rag.
00124242 ....$9.99

ROMANTIC INSPIRATIONS

Early Advanced Level
From "Arabesque" to "Nocturne" to "Rapsodie," the inspired pieces in this collection are a perfect choice for students who want to play beautiful, expressive and impressive literature at the recital. Includes: Arabesque • Journey's End • Nocturne • Nocturne d'Esprit • Prelude No. 1 • Rapsodie • Rondo Capriccioso • Valse d'Automne.
00296813...$8.99

SUMMERTIME FUN

Elementary Level
Twelve terrific originals from favorite HLSPL composers, all at the elementary level. Songs: Accidental Wizard • Butterflies and Rainbows • Chill Out! • Down by the Lake • The Enchanted Mermaid • Gone Fishin' • The Merry Merry-Go-Round • Missing You • Pink Lemonade • Rockin' the Boat • Teeter-Totter • Wind Chimes.
00296831 ....$7.99